FOOTBALL
RECORD BREAKERS

By Aaron Jonathan Gray

SportsZone
An Imprint of Abdo Publishing | abdopublishing.com

abdopublishing.com

Published by Abdo Publishing, a division of ABDO, PO Box 398166, Minneapolis, Minnesota 55439. Copyright © 2016 by Abdo Consulting Group, Inc. International copyrights reserved in all countries. No part of this book may be reproduced in any form without written permission from the publisher. SportsZone™ is a trademark and logo of Abdo Publishing.

Printed in the United States of America, North Mankato, Minnesota
032015
092015

**THIS BOOK CONTAINS
RECYCLED MATERIALS**

Cover Photo: Joe Mahoney/AP Images, cover (left); Andrew Innerarity/AP Images, cover (right)
Interior Photos: Joe Mahoney/AP Images, 1 (left), 14; Andrew Innerarity/AP Images, 1 (right), 17; Tim Sharp/AP Images 5; Eric Gay/AP Images, 7; Tony Gutierrez/AP Images, 8; Lenny Ignlezi/AP Images, 11; Brennan Linsley/AP Images, 12; George Rose/Getty Images, 18; Phil Sandlin/AP Images, 20; AP Images, 23, 27, 28; Jim Boudier/AP Images, 24; Mark Humphrey/AP Images, 31; Nick Wass/AP Images, 32; Ricky Carioti/AP Images, 35; Amy E. Conn/AP Images, 36; Charles Agel/AP Images, 39; John J. Gaps III/AP Images, 41; Miles Kennedy/AP Images, 42; John Stewart/AP Images, 44; John Storey/AP Images, 45

Editor: Patrick Donnelly
Series Designer: Nikki Farinella

Library of Congress Control Number: 2015931684

Cataloging-in-Publication Data
Gray, Aaron Jonathan.
 Football record breakers / Aaron Jonathon Gray.
  p. cm. -- (Record breakers)
Includes bibliographical references and index.
ISBN 978-1-62403-847-1
1. Football--Juvenile literature. 2. Football--Records--Juvenile literature.
I. Title.
796.332--dc23
                                                          2015931684

TABLE OF CONTENTS

Note: All records in this book are current through the 2014 NFL season.

1
RELENTLESS RUNNER

Emmitt Smith was comfortable with a target on his back. In fact, he thrived on the attention his opponents gave him.

During his 15-year National Football League (NFL) career, Smith was usually the focus of opposing defenses whenever he stepped onto the field. Game plans were designed to shut him down. All 11 defenders wanted a piece of him. Football is a physical, brutal sport, and Smith's body took a beating every week.

Emmitt Smith, *front*, played 13 of his 15 NFL seasons in Dallas, where he piled up rushing yards while leading the Cowboys to three Super Bowl titles.

But the Dallas Cowboys' star running back was not intimidated. Instead, he kept coming back for more. Smith was an expert at waiting for his blockers to open a hole at the line of scrimmage. Then he would burst past the first wave of defenders. He kept his powerful legs churning as would-be tacklers bounced aside. He shrugged off other defenders with shifty moves and vicious stiff-arms. Then he used his speed to break into the clear.

Smith became one of the most reliable running backs ever to play the game. Over 13 years in Dallas and two with the Arizona Cardinals, he carried the ball almost 20 times per game. And he rarely missed a game. That consistency helped him finish his career with 18,355 rushing yards, more than any player in NFL history. Smith also tops the league's career list with 164 rushing touchdowns and 4,409 carries. And he helped lead the Cowboys to three Super Bowl titles in the 1990s.

By 2002, the Cowboys' dynasty was over. They were on their way to a third straight losing season. But they still had Smith taking aim at Walter Payton's all-time rushing record. He was 93 yards behind Payton when the Seattle Seahawks came to town on October 27, 2002.

The game began like so many others before. Smith got the ball on the Cowboys' first three offensive plays. The game plan was to establish the ground game early and let Smith wear down the defense with his punishing runs.

Emmitt Smith slashes through the San Francisco 49ers defense in the National Football Conference (NFC) Championship game on January 23, 1994.

With 10 minutes to play, Smith was just 13 yards away from tying the record. The Cowboys took over at their own 27-yard line. The fans rose to their feet, sensing history in the making. On first down, Smith plunged ahead for three yards. On second down, he took care of the rest.

Emmitt Smith celebrates after breaking the NFL record for career rushing yards on October 27, 2002.

Smith took the handoff, burst off left tackle, fit his way through a small hole, and cut left. He briefly stumbled over the arm of an opponent, but he kept his balance and chugged ahead for an 11-yard gain.

When Smith bounced back onto his feet, he knew the record was his. He took off his helmet and took a knee. Then he pointed to the sky to honor the late Payton, who had owned the all-time rushing record for nearly two decades before that day.

Smith played only eight more games for the Cowboys. He played his last two seasons with the Cardinals, tacking on almost 1,200 more yards to set the bar even higher for the next challenger. But it would take a special player to break Smith's record—a player willing to take the ball, even when every player on the field knew he would. That player would have to be strong enough to take those hits and keep coming back, week after week. A player like Smith does not come around very often.

SANDERS'S AMAZING STREAK

BARRY SANDERS WAS ALREADY A SUPERSTAR BY 1997. BUT IN HIS FIRST TWO GAMES THAT SEASON HE GAINED JUST 53 YARDS. THEN SANDERS TOOK OFF. HE RUSHED FOR AT LEAST 100 YARDS IN HIS NEXT 14 GAMES. THAT SET AN NFL RECORD FOR MOST CONSECUTIVE 100-YARD RUSHING GAMES. SANDERS FINISHED THAT SEASON WITH 2,053 RUSHING YARDS ON 335 CARRIES. HE AVERAGED 6.1 YARDS PER CARRY AND 128.3 YARDS PER GAME. HE ALSO BECAME ONLY THE THIRD PLAYER TO REACH 2,000 YARDS IN A SINGLE SEASON.

2
PASSING
KING

Peyton Manning did not miss a start during his first 13 years with the Indianapolis Colts. But when a neck injury sidelined him for the entire 2011 season, his future was in doubt. Manning had been one of the best quarterbacks in the league. He put up big numbers and won big games. He won the NFL Most Valuable Player (MVP) award four times in Indianapolis.

Manning was finally ready to play again in 2012. But the Colts were ready to move on. They released their longtime star and replaced him with rookie Andrew Luck. Would Manning's career be over at the age of 36?

Peyton Manning was a four-time NFL MVP during his 13 years with the Indianapolis Colts.

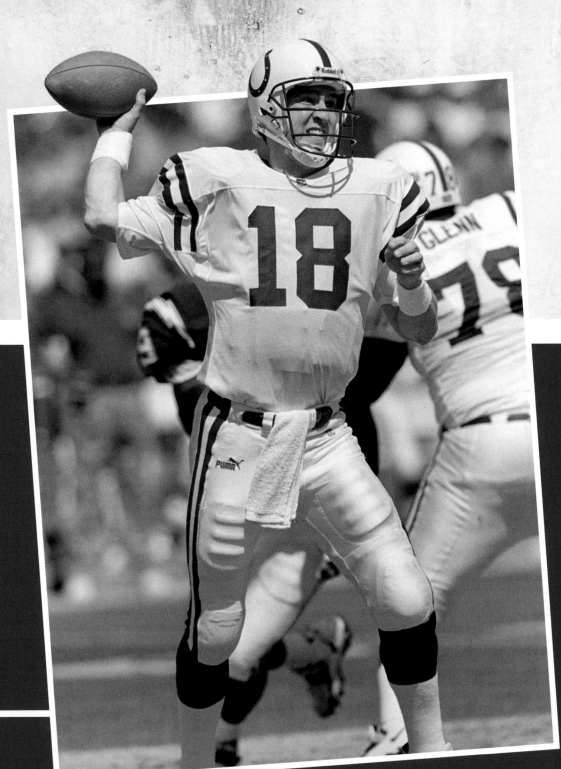

Far from it. Manning was not blessed with the strongest arm. He also was never the fastest runner. But he never let another player outwork him. He studied defenses until he knew all of their weaknesses. And he used his accurate passing to tear them apart. He was not going to let his career end without a fight.

Manning signed with the Denver Broncos. After getting back into form in 2012, he began playing the best football of his life. In 2013 he passed for 5,477 yards and 55 touchdowns, both single-season NFL records. He led the Broncos to the Super Bowl that year. Then he came back in 2014 to break the record for most career passing touchdowns in the NFL.

His 509th touchdown pass came on October 19, 2014. It was a warm night in Colorado. The fans buzzed with excitement as they filed into the stadium to watch the Broncos take on the San Francisco 49ers. Manning needed just three touchdown passes to overtake Brett Favre atop the career touchdown list. Three touchdowns in one game was no stretch for Manning. He had already done that four times in the season's first five games.

Manning quickly let the fans know they were about to see history. The 49ers were having a hard time covering his wide receivers. On the Broncos' opening drive Manning connected with Emmanuel Sanders for a 3-yard touchdown.

Wide receiver Emmanuel Sanders, *left*, flips the ball to a teammate in a playful game of keep-away after Peyton Manning, *right*, broke the NFL record for career touchdown passes.

Denver Broncos fans celebrate Peyton Manning's record-breaking touchdown pass on October 19, 2014.

Manning tied the record later in the first quarter when he hit Wes Welker for a 39-yard score.

The record-breaker came on an 8-yard touchdown pass to Demaryius Thomas with 3:09 left in the second quarter. But the fun was just beginning. Thomas, Welker, Sanders, and tight end Julius Thomas played keep-away with the record-breaking ball. They tossed it back and forth over Manning's head as the quarterback laughed. It was a unique celebration for a unique player.

The record highlighted how remarkably efficient Manning had been during his career. It took him only 246 games to break a mark that took Favre 302 games to set. He finished the 2014 season with 39 touchdown passes. It was only the fourth time that he had thrown more than 33 in a season. In fact, three of those years were his first three in Denver. Most players slow down with age. In Denver, Manning showed he was an exception to that rule.

FAVRE'S IRONMAN STREAK

BRETT FAVRE STARTED AT QUARTERBACK FOR THE GREEN BAY PACKERS ON SEPTEMBER 27, 1992. HE THEN STARTED EVERY WEEK FOR MORE THAN 18 YEARS. THE STREAK CONTINUED EVEN AFTER HE JOINED THE NEW YORK JETS AND THEN THE MINNESOTA VIKINGS. A SPRAINED SHOULDER FINALLY KEPT HIM OUT OF A GAME ON DECEMBER 13, 2010, SNAPPING HIS STREAK AT 297 CONSECUTIVE STARTS. DURING THE STREAK, FAVRE FOUGHT THROUGH BROKEN BONES, ACHES AND PAINS, AND PERSONAL GRIEF TO PLAY WEEK AFTER WEEK. HE STARTED ONE GAME THE DAY AFTER HIS FATHER DIED. IN HIS 20-YEAR CAREER, THE THREE-TIME NFL MVP WON ONE SUPER BOWL AND WAS SELECTED TO THE PRO BOWL 11 TIMES.

3
PRACTICE
MAKES PERFECT

Rain poured down on Candlestick Park on December 6, 1992. But Jerry Rice was not going to let that spoil his day.

One week earlier, the San Francisco 49ers' star wide receiver had made his 100th touchdown catch. That tied the NFL career record held by Steve Largent. The former Seattle Seahawks great needed 14 seasons to do it. Now Rice, in just his eighth NFL season, was ready to write his name into the history books.

Jerry Rice was a three-time Super Bowl champion and a record-setting wide receiver for the San Francisco 49ers.

The Niners were hosting the Miami Dolphins. In the fourth quarter Rice and his teammates lined up at the Miami 12-yard line. Looking across the line of scrimmage, Rice saw J. B. Brown was covering him. Rice ran straight at Brown, getting the Miami cornerback on his heels. Then he cut hard to his right, continuing the slant pattern to the goal line. Quarterback Steve Young delivered the pass on target. Brown was helpless to stop it. Rice had the record.

The Niners mobbed Rice in the end zone. Then they ran off the field together as Rice thrust the ball over his head as he had so many times before.

Rice's entire career is proof that practice makes perfect. When he arrived in San Francisco in 1985, Rice wanted to make a good first impression on his new teammates. He did it by treating each practice like it was a game. After every catch, whether he was five or 95 yards away, Rice would sprint all the way to the end zone. It became a famous practice habit that Rice used throughout his 20-year career. But back in 1985, it raised a few eyebrows among the 49ers veterans.

The speedy wide receiver quickly won them over. Rice seemed to have a motor that never stopped. His steady practice habits helped him become one of the most consistent wide receivers on the team.

Jerry Rice beats Miami Dolphins cornerback J. B. Brown for his 101st career touchdown reception on December 6, 1992.

Jerry Rice hauls in a pass in the fourth quarter of the Super Bowl on January 22, 1989. Rice was named the game's MVP as the 49ers beat the Cincinnati Bengals.

Rice caught only three touchdown passes during his rookie season. But he exploded onto the scene in his second year with 15 touchdown receptions. That was the first of 10 straight seasons in which Rice scored at least

10 touchdowns. In 1987 Rice caught 22 touchdown passes in just 12 games. That was a single-season record that stood for 20 years. In the 1988 and 1989 seasons, Rice helped lead San Francisco to two Super Bowl titles.

In his first Super Bowl, Rice displayed his toughness and reliability. Just six days before the game, he reinjured his ankle, which had been sore for weeks. But he did not lose a step. Rice caught 11 passes for 215 yards and a touchdown. He was rewarded with the Super Bowl MVP honors as the Niners beat the Cincinnati Bengals 20–16.

Rice won three Super Bowl titles with San Francisco and set countless records. But his tireless work ethic and durability made him one of the greatest players of all time.

MOSS THE BOSS

IN HIS TENTH NFL SEASON, RANDY MOSS JOINED THE NEW ENGLAND PATRIOTS. IT DID NOT TAKE LONG FOR HIM AND QUARTERBACK TOM BRADY TO MAKE HISTORY. THE 2007 PATRIOTS WENT 16–0 IN THE REGULAR SEASON, AND MOSS WAS A BIG PART OF THAT SUCCESS. MOSS CAUGHT 23 TOUCHDOWN PASSES THAT YEAR, BREAKING JERRY RICE'S SINGLE-SEASON RECORD SET 20 YEARS EARLIER. MOSS'S RECORD-BREAKING CATCH CAME IN THE LAST GAME OF THE SEASON. THE PATRIOTS NEEDED TO BEAT THE NEW YORK GIANTS TO FINISH THEIR PERFECT REGULAR SEASON. BRADY FOUND MOSS STREAKING DOWN THE RIGHT SIDELINE FOR A 65-YARD TOUCHDOWN PASS IN THE FOURTH QUARTER. IT PUT THE PATRIOTS AHEAD FOR GOOD IN A 38–35 VICTORY.

4

THE MIAMI
MIRACLE

Rarely does a 38-year-old backup quarterback make a big difference in a football team's season. But Earl Morrall did so in 1972. He helped the Miami Dolphins become the only NFL team to go undefeated and win the Super Bowl.

Dolphins coach Don Shula knew Morrall well. Four years earlier, Morrall led Shula's Baltimore Colts to the Super Bowl and was named the NFL MVP. Shula eventually started a new dynasty in Miami. And before the 1972 season, he brought in Morrall as a backup.

Coach Don Shula, *left,* and quarterback Earl Morrall chat during the Miami Dolphins' perfect 1972 season.

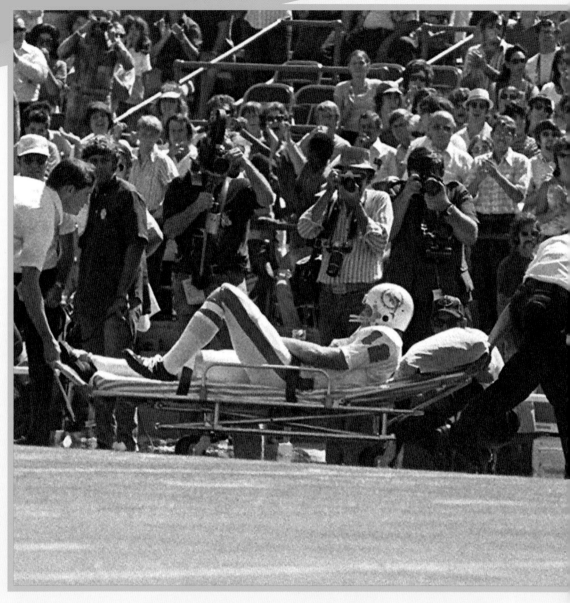

Miami Dolphins quarterback Bob Griese is taken from the field on a stretcher with a broken leg on October 15, 1972, leaving veteran Earl Morrall to carry the Dolphins to an undefeated season.

Morrall was little more than an insurance policy. After all, the Dolphins had Bob Griese entering the prime of his career. The 27-year-old quarterback had led the

1971 Dolphins to a 10–3–1 record and their first Super Bowl appearance.

Miami also had a fantastic rushing attack, a top-ranked defense, and one of the best coaches in NFL history. And as the Dolphins won their first four games, Morrall was little more than a cheerleader on the sidelines.

But Griese went down with a broken leg in Week 5 against the San Diego Chargers. Suddenly the whole season was on Morrall's back. The veteran had already been a backup to Hall of Fame quarterbacks Fran Tarkenton and Johnny Unitas. But as he marched onto the field against the Chargers he was still unknown in Miami.

His years of experience helped him figure out just how to make his young teammates comfortable. Offensive lineman Bob Kuechenberg recalled how Morrall broke the ice when he entered that first huddle.

"All right," Morrall said. "Anyone know any dirty jokes?"

With the tension eased, Morrall threw two touchdown passes that day. The Dolphins cruised to a 24–10 victory. Their passing game, it appeared, was in good hands.

But there was much more to that Dolphins team than just its quarterback. Its offense relied on a power running game that featured the amazing trio of Larry Csonka, Jim Kiick, and Mercury Morris. Together they rushed for more than 2,500 yards that season. Those Dolphins became the first team to have two 1,000-yard rushers (Csonka and Morris) in the same backfield.

But what happened on the other side of the ball was pretty special, too. Miami's defense had a catchy—and fitting—nickname. The Dolphins and Dallas Cowboys had played in the Super Bowl a year earlier. Dallas coach Tom Landry was asked a question about the Miami defense, which had allowed only 174 points in the regular season. Landry said, "I can't recall their names, but they are a matter of great concern to us."

From that point forward, defensive coordinator Bill Arnsparger's troops became known as the "No-Name Defense." They did not have many stars, but during their perfect run in 1972 they took their rightful place among the best in NFL history.

Defensive end Vern Den Herder, defensive tackle Manny Fernandez, and linebacker Nick Buoniconti led the Miami defense. Individually they were not big names. But as a unit they allowed the fewest yards and points in the NFL that year. Four of those defensive players were selected for the Pro Bowl.

The defense posted three shutouts over the last eight games of the regular season as Morrall and the Dolphins charged into the playoffs. Miami beat the Cleveland Browns 20–14 in its first playoff game. Even though the Dolphins were undefeated, thanks to a rule that has since been changed, they had to play the American Football

Miami Dolphins running back Larry Csonka, *right*, outruns Pittsburgh Steelers linebacker Andy Russell to score a touchdown in the AFC Championship Game.

Miami players carry head coach Don Shula, *center*, off the field after the Dolphins completed an undefeated season with a 14–7 win over the Washington Redskins in the Super Bowl on January 14, 1973.

Conference (AFC) championship on the road. By then Griese was healthy, and he returned to action midway through a 21–17 win over the Pittsburgh Steelers.

Griese started the Super Bowl against the Washington Redskins on January 14, 1973. The defense did not surrender a touchdown, and the offense did enough to lead the way to a 14–7 victory. The win capped off a 17–0 season for the Dolphins. Then they won another Super Bowl the next season.

But it's the 1972 Dolphins that live in history. They remain the only team to play an entire season without a loss and win the Super Bowl.

ALMOST PERFECT

IN 2007 THE NEW ENGLAND PATRIOTS WENT TWO GAMES BEYOND THE DOLPHINS' FEAT, BUT THEY COULD NOT FINISH THE JOB. A DEADLY OFFENSIVE ATTACK AVERAGED ALMOST 37 POINTS A GAME AS THE PATRIOTS WENT 16–0 IN THE REGULAR SEASON. SINCE THE SUPER BOWL ERA BEGAN IN 1966, ONLY THE 1972 DOLPHINS HAD PREVIOUSLY COMPLETED AN UNDEFEATED REGULAR SEASON (ALTHOUGH THE SEASON WAS ONLY 14 GAMES UNTIL 1978). NEW ENGLAND THEN BEAT THE JACKSONVILLE JAGUARS AND THE SAN DIEGO CHARGERS IN ITS FIRST TWO PLAYOFF GAMES. TALK OF THE PATRIOTS MATCHING THE '72 DOLPHINS' PERFECT NFL SEASON STARTED TO GET LOUDER. BUT IN THE SUPER BOWL, THE NEW YORK GIANTS SCORED A LATE TOUCHDOWN TO SHOCK THE PATRIOTS 17–14. NEW ENGLAND HAD TO SETTLE FOR 18–1.

5

LEWIS
LEADS RAVENS D

The NFL started changing some of its rules during the 1990s. League officials knew fans loved seeing high-scoring games. Star quarterbacks, running backs, and receivers became the biggest names in the game. Defense, it appeared, was yesterday's news. So the league changed some rules to make it harder to play defense.

Offensive numbers started exploding. But in 2000, the Baltimore Ravens reminded fans that having a dominant defense was still possible. The Ravens defense brought a Super Bowl title to Baltimore and set a number of NFL records along the way.

Baltimore Ravens defensive tackles Tony Siragusa, *left*, and Sam Adams, *right*, swallow up Tennessee Titans running back Eddie George.

Middle linebacker Ray Lewis, defensive tackle Tony Siragusa, and safety Rod Woodson led Baltimore's punishing defense. The Ravens allowed just 165 points and 970 rushing yards. Both are records for a 16-game season. They also held a record 11 opponents to 10 or fewer points in a game.

But the Ravens' offense was not making it easy on the defense. After Baltimore whipped the Cincinnati Bengals 37–0 in Week 4, the Ravens did not score another touchdown for the next five games. Remarkably, Baltimore still managed to win two of those five games. It helped that the defense held opponents to a five-game total of just 43 points.

The Ravens' offense regained a pulse in a 27–7 win at Cincinnati in Week 10. After that, Baltimore did not lose another game. The Ravens ended the regular season on a seven-game winning streak, then bulldozed four postseason opponents. Their remarkable run peaked on January 28, 2001, with a 34–7 Super Bowl victory over the New York Giants.

Ravens head coach Brian Billick might have seen the writing on the wall in the preseason. He entered the year with a simple motto: "The best offense for a football team is a good defense." He knew his team did not have a lot of firepower on offense. Journeymen Trent Dilfer

Middle linebacker Ray Lewis was the heart and soul of the Baltimore Ravens' record-setting defense in 2000.

and Tony Banks were splitting time at quarterback. Their starting running back was rookie Jamal Lewis.

That put the focus on Baltimore's defense. Its leader was Ray Lewis, who was in his fifth NFL season and just starting to enter his prime. Defensive coordinator Marvin Lewis ran a basic 4–3 defensive scheme. That meant he had four linemen and three linebackers. It was designed to stop the run and free up Ray Lewis to make plays all over the field.

While Ray Lewis roamed the middle of the field and called the defensive plays, he got plenty of help from the rest of the defense. On the line, Siragusa and Sam Adams combined to form a wall in the middle. On the edges, Michael McCrary, Peter Boulware, and Rob Burnett provided constant pressure on the quarterback. Woodson, a future Hall of Famer, commanded the secondary while first-round draft picks Chris McAlister and Duane Starks turned interceptions into touchdowns.

Once Baltimore reached the playoffs, the defense *really* took over. The Ravens allowed just one offensive touchdown in four postseason games. Not one per game—one total, in four games. No team in the history of the league had put together such a dominant postseason run.

The Ravens' performance in the Super Bowl was one for the ages. Baltimore's stingy secondary picked off four passes and the defense forced the Giants to punt 11 times.

Defense was a team effort for the Baltimore Ravens in 2000, as Cincinnati Bengals running back Clif Groce, *center*, discovered on this play.

35

Baltimore coach Brian Billick is doused with Gatorade as the Ravens wrapped up their Super Bowl victory over the New York Giants on January 28, 2001.

New York's only score came on a kickoff return in the third quarter.

Ray Lewis provided a fairytale ending to the 2000 season by being named the Super Bowl MVP. The award completed a season in which he also won the NFL Defensive Player of the Year and was named a Pro Bowl starter and a first-team All-Pro.

The Ravens might not have lit up the scoreboard, but Billick's motto proved true. The best offense for the 2000 Baltimore Ravens was their dominating defense.

THE STEEL CURTAIN

AFTER STARTING THE 1976 SEASON 1–4, THE PITTSBURGH STEELERS RELIED ON ITS DEFENSE TO TURN THINGS AROUND. NICKNAMED "THE STEEL CURTAIN," THE STEELERS' DEFENSE CLAMPED DOWN IN A BIG WAY. OVER THE NEXT NINE GAMES, PITTSBURGH'S OPPONENTS SCORED A COMBINED 28 POINTS. THE STEELERS SET A MODERN NFL RECORD WITH FIVE SHUTOUTS ALONG THE WAY. LINEBACKERS JACK LAMBERT AND JACK HAM WERE NAMED FIRST-TEAM ALL-PRO, WHILE ALL FOUR DEFENSIVE BACKS AND TWO DEFENSIVE LINEMEN WERE NAMED TO THE PRO BOWL.

6
SACK
MASTER SMITH

For 15 years, defensive end Bruce Smith was a beast for the Buffalo Bills. His tenacious drive to get the sack struck fear into every quarterback in the league. And his powerful play even helped the Bills reach four straight Super Bowls.

But it was during his later years, when playing for the Washington Redskins, that Smith secured his place in history. Smith entered the 2003 season with 195 sacks. Only Reggie White had more. The longtime Philadelphia Eagles and Green Bay Packers star had retired three years earlier with 198 sacks. That meant Smith needed just four more to set the record.

Buffalo Bills defensive end Bruce Smith sacks New England Patriots quarterback Drew Bledsoe in 1996.

At age 40, Smith's career was winding down. Meanwhile, the Redskins had missed the playoffs the previous two years and were struggling again in 2003. Because of that, Smith found himself in a backup role with the team. But everyone still watched as he crept up on the sacks milestone.

Some Bills thought the record would fall in Week 7. The Redskins played in Buffalo. Smith came into the game just two sacks shy of the record. Old teammates even showed up for the possible record-breaking moment and Smith homecoming. Instead, the Bills cruised to a 24–7 victory, and Smith saw limited action.

The record would have to wait, but time had always been on Smith's side. He was the first overall pick in the 1985 NFL Draft. For 19 years, he excelled due to both his amazing athleticism and his dedication to studying the game. During his career, and even more so during his later years, Smith would watch hours of video each week. He honed his craft and searched for weaknesses on opposing offensive lines.

Smith was starting to show his age during the 2003 season. It would be his last in the NFL. He was nearly old enough to be the father of some of the players he was going up against. But after almost two decades in the NFL, he was still intent on turning the corner, getting stronger, and adding a few more sacks to his career tally.

Smith recorded a sack in Week 9 against the Seattle Seahawks. Two weeks later he shared a sack with

Bruce Smith spent 15 years terrorizing quarterbacks for the Buffalo Bills.

Renaldo Wynn against the Miami Dolphins. Now he was tied with White. With the record in his sights, Smith was a man on a mission.

Two weeks later, on December 7, 2003, the Redskins went on the road to play the New York Giants. Early in the game, Smith laid a hard hit on Kerry Collins. It knocked the Giants' starting quarterback out of the game. But Smith was not done yet. He was matched up against 25-year-old offensive lineman Ian Allen of the Giants. The veteran must have seen plenty of weaknesses to exploit during that week's video session. He beat the younger Allen on just about every play.

The record-breaking sack was typical Smith. It was a result of the cleverness and physical prowess he had shown the league for years. At 6-foot-4 and 262 pounds, Smith still had all the quickness that helped him get elected to the

Bruce Smith, *right*, takes down Philadelphia Eagles quarterback Donovan McNabb in 2003.

Pro Bowl 11 times. Allen had no chance. With Smith bearing down on the record, not many offensive linemen could have contained him. On the record-breaking play, Smith beat Allen on the inside and smothered backup quarterback Jesse Palmer.

All of Smith's teammates rushed onto the field to congratulate him. When Smith got back to the locker room, he found a box from his tailor. Off the field, Smith was known for his love of comfort. During his down time, he liked to lounge in bathrobes and just relax. At the beginning of the season, his tailor had given him the box. Washington's locker-room staff held onto it. The tailor had just one simple request: the box could only be opened after Smith became the league's new sack king.

Finally, Smith opened the tailor's box. He found a custom-made robe in Redskins colors. On the front, in script, were the words *All Time*. On the back was a Redskins logo. Smith recorded one more sack that year to finish with 200 in his career. He retired after the season, finally satisfied that he was the NFL's sack king.

STRAHAN'S SUCCESS

MICHAEL STRAHAN'S SINGLE-SEASON SACK RECORD IS NOT ALWAYS REMEMBERED FONDLY. ON JANUARY 6, 2002, STRAHAN'S NEW YORK GIANTS HOSTED THE GREEN BAY PACKERS. THE PACKERS HELD A FIRM LEAD LATE IN THE GAME. THEN, WITH LESS THAN THREE MINUTES REMAINING, THE DEFENSIVE END BROKE FREE OFF THE LEFT EDGE AND FELL ON TOP OF A SLIDING BRETT FAVRE. SOME THOUGHT FAVRE GAVE UP ON THE PLAY, ALLOWING HIS FRIEND STRAHAN TO SACK HIM. EITHER WAY, STRAHAN WAS CREDITED WITH SACK NUMBER 22.5 OF THE 2001 SEASON. THAT SET THE NFL RECORD FOR MOST SACKS IN A SEASON. SACKS HAD ONLY BEEN KEPT AS AN OFFICIAL STATISTIC SINCE 1982. THE NEW YORK JETS' MARK GASTINEAU HELD THE PREVIOUS RECORD OF 22. STRAHAN SPENT HIS ENTIRE 14-YEAR CAREER WITH THE GIANTS. HE HELPED THE TEAM WIN THE SUPER BOWL AFTER THE 2007 SEASON, WHICH WAS HIS FINAL YEAR IN THE NFL. STRAHAN WAS ELECTED TO THE PRO BOWL SEVEN TIMES.

FUN FACTS

TOUCHDOWN TRIO

What do running back Walter Payton, *below*, and wide receiver David Patten have in common? They were each responsible for three touchdowns in a game—the hard way. They each rushed for a touchdown, caught a touchdown pass, and threw a touchdown pass. Payton did it for the Chicago Bears in 1979. Patten pulled it off with the New England Patriots in 2001.

MASSIVE MAN

Michael Jasper weighed 448 pounds when he was drafted by the Buffalo Bills in 2011. He was the biggest player ever to wear an NFL uniform. The offensive lineman and nose tackle dwarfed his teammates. But he also had a vertical jump of 32 inches and could dunk a basketball.

TURNOVER TERROR

Who had the worst game in NFL history? It might be Chicago Cardinals quarterback Jim Hardy. During the first game of the 1950 season, Hardy threw eight interceptions, which is still an NFL record.

RESPECT YOUR ELDERS

NO SUPER BOWL GLORY

Of the NFL's 32 teams, 28 of them have made it to a Super Bowl. The Houston Texans, Jacksonville Jaguars, Detroit Lions, and Cleveland Browns are the only teams that have been left out.

Legendary quarterback and kicker George Blanda, *above*, began playing pro football in 1949. He finally retired in 1975 at age 48. He played 26 seasons, which is a league record. He is one of only two players to play in four different decades. He also holds the record for most extra points kicked in a career with 943.

GLOSSARY

coordinator
An assistant coach who is in charge of the offense or defense.

draft
The process by which leagues determine which teams can sign new players coming into the league.

dynasty
A long stretch of dominance over many years by one team.

fumble
When a player loses control of the football.

journeyman
A player who has played for many teams.

line of scrimmage
The place on the field where a play starts.

Pro Bowl
The NFL's All-Star game, in which the best players in the league compete.

rookie
A player in his first year in the league.

sack
When the quarterback is tackled behind the line of scrimmage before he can throw the ball.

upset
When a supposedly weaker team beats a stronger team.

veteran
A player who has played many years.

FOR MORE INFORMATION

Gitlin, Marty. *Peyton Manning: Superstar Quarterback.*
   Minneapolis, MN: Abdo Publishing, 2011.

Graves, Will. *The Best NFL Defenses of All Time.* Minneapolis, MN:
   Abdo Publishing, 2014.

McMahon, Dave. *Miami Dolphins.* Minneapolis, MN:
   Abdo Publishing, 2011.

WEBSITES

To learn more about Record Breakers, visit
booklinks.abdopublishing.com. These links are routinely
monitored and updated to provide the most current
information available.

PLACE TO VISIT

Pro Football Hall of Fame
2121 George Halas Drive NW
Canton, Ohio 44708
(330) 456-8207
www.profootballhof.com
Built in 1963, the Pro Football Hall of Fame celebrates the best
football players ever to play the game. Up to seven inductees
are enshrined each year. The purpose of the hall is to honor the
heroes of the game, preserve its history, promote its values, and
celebrate its excellence.

INDEX

ABOUT THE AUTHOR

Aaron Jonathan Gray grew up in Herndon, Virginia, and graduated from James Madison University with a degree in Specialized Media Arts and Design. He has won several Associated Press Sports Editors awards for breaking news and production design during his career as a professional sports journalist. He lives with his wife in Abu Dhabi, United Arab Emirates.